SEEDS OF AWAKENING
SPIRITUAL AND PSYCHIC DEVELOPMENT SUPPORT GUIDE BOOK

A self-help guidebook is intended to assist those who are now beginning to experience Spiritual and Psychic events in their lives, as well as for those who are Re-Awakening and Re-membering their Path of Self Realization in this lifetime.

My hope is that this guidebook will serve to point the way towards additional resources and information, whether Spiritual or Psychic, that can give you more in depth information or experiential assistance to guide you along the Way Back to Source.

This guidebook includes information gathered while I was in the process of preparing my lessons and in teaching Spiritual and Psychic Development as well as Energy Clearing, Meditation, the use of Mantras and The Sight and Sounds of Spirit.

You may contact me with your comments and/or questions at www.findpeacewithin.com.

INTRODUCTION

I have created this book to assist others in finding answers to their initial questions as they open to Spirit. May you have a blessed journey as you begin to "see" Spirit manifest in your life.

I feel very strongly that it is not enough to practice developing our Psychic Skills, but we must also practice developing our Spiritual Connection with God, Source, Divine Father/ Mother through whatever means is comfortable for us.

I believe that Psychic development is only a stepping stone to that 'Real' Spiritual Connection, that 'Real' Connection with God, The God Source that resides within each one of us.

It is my hope that you will find some of the suggestions in this Psychic and Spiritual development Guidebook helpful to you in obtaining balance as you Re-Member with your Higher Self, that Higher aspect of you that is connected with The God Source, this Higher Aspect of you that is in direct communication with your personal self here in this life. We have only to open and become aware of this Guidance.

My studies have been very eclectic as I have advanced on my Path of Re-Membrance, of Enlightenment, of Freedom. I am always open to learn from the many Ascended Masters and guides who are here to help us as we " Re-Awaken" to our Selves.

"I pray that the Infinite Father-Mother-Friend-God becomes a living enlightening Presence in our lives– bringing strength, guidance, renewal and healing."
Sri Daya Mata, successor to Yogananda

Table of Contents

Chapter One

Spiritual and Psychic Experiences

WHO CAN I TALK TO ABOUT MY SPIRITUAL AND PSYCHIC EXPERIENCES?

**You can always seek help in the many
Spiritual and Psychic Development Support Circles**

A SPIRITUAL and PSYCHIC DEVELOPMENT SUPPORT CIRCLE consists of a group of people who gather together to share the experiences that they have had with Spirit. It is where people from all walks of life come together to share their experiences with Spirit, gain valuable information to further their journey and offer and receive support from one another and from Spirit.

These Circles exist to allow you to feel comfortable and secure sharing your experiences with other like-minded people. They are also a place in which to meditate, to allow you to practice your new skills. They are also a space to clear your chakra energy systems and to experience healing, guidance and wisdom from our own Inner Guides.

During a Development Circle session you may experience meditations, energy clearings and many other activities to assist in fine tuning your communication skills with Your Higher Self, Your Guides and with Source.

You are free to explore how and why Spirit is trying to gain your attention. You can learn and practice the many benefits of 'Going Within' during meditation. You can share your experiences and gain validation from each other and Spirit.

Visit or call your local New Age/Metaphysical Store for a Spiritual and Psychic Development Support Circle near you or feel free to contact me, Gerri DeSimone at www.findpeacewithin.com for a listing of suggested locations for Support Circles.

Go Within

"Go Within and you will 'SEE'
ALL that you are meant to see.
You will find that You are Well
and that all illusion causes so much of this hell.

But in Truth and Light this all does fade
For as you Go Within your connection is made.
Your Connection with the Source of you
that filters through All the rest, unto.

Find this place of Love Inside
and rest within there all the Time.
Keep yourself engaged on earth
but truly settled within your Birth.

The Birthing that I say unto
is the Birthing of the Likes of you.
The Likes of you that does Truly SEE
The All within All that BE."
Via Gerri

Chapter Two

The Four Major Psychic Senses

THE FOUR 'CLAIRS'

Clairsentience

Clairsentience or Psychic Feeling may be the most readily noticed psychic sensation of the body.
The location of this 'Psychic Feeling' is most often on the front of the physical body in the area called the solar plexus. This area is just above the waist line on the physical body. It is the place where you are most likely to experience those 'gut feelings' or 'gut instincts' about certain people, places and situations. It is that 'funny feeling' that tells you that something is not quite right, or that something feels just right.

Clair cognizance

Clair cognizance or 'knowing' **can** be more difficult to differentiate as you must begin to learn to trust in yourself. Claircognizance is an inner awareness, a 'knowingness' – for some reason you simply can't explain. You just know the information requested. You just know the answer to the question being asked, You just know!!

The location of this psychic intuition is the crown and top of your head. It is the place where we connect with the Wisdom of The Universe. This center of psychic intuition, of knowing, extends upwards and serves to conduct life force energy and guidance into the brain.

Bring your awareness upwards and just observe your impressions, try not to concentrate, just contemplate.

You will see this skill begin to manifest when you have the experience of knowing what someone will say before they speak or knowing who is on the telephone before you pick up the phone or even knowing the answer to a particular question without knowing how you know this information!

Clairaudience

Clairaudience is also known as Psychic Hearing. This manifests as 'hearing voices' in your head.

The location of Psychic Hearing is on each side of the head, just above your ears. The section of the brain that is associated with auditory processing is located in this area.

Clairaudience presents itself as a stream of inner consciousness. This can manifest as a stream of words, phrases or music. Perhaps even the actual sounds are heard outside of the head.

Spirit can communicate with you through these impressions of various sounds and words. It may take some time to acquire the ability to discern as to "Who is speaking?", "Do I hear myself or my Guidance?"
That differentiation of sounds does come through continued Practice with this skill.

Clairvoyance

Clairvoyance also known as 'seeing' and can take on many forms of 'seeing'.

The location for clairvoyance is in the Third Eye which is located at the center of your forehead, just above and between your eyebrows.
You can easily begin to practice 'Seeing' simply by closing your eyes and bringing your awareness upward to this area on your forehead called the 'Third Eye'.

Sometimes you 'See' with your eyes open and sometimes with your eyes closed. This seeing can be described as if 'seeing' a memory in your mind. Take a moment to think about your home and you can 'see' this in your mind's eye. This is a form of psychic 'Seeing' and gives you an example of what someone who has practiced with their psychic senses mean when they say, "I See…"

There are many different ways to experience clairvoyance with some people actually seeing Spirits as Energy orbs or bright lights.

Another way is to see the brightly colored Auras and energy patterns that are located around every living thing. By seeing the colors and shapes of an individual aura, you are given further insight into the state of another's energy field. What we can see with the help of aura photography can be seen by many without the photography equipment.

Another way to experience Clairvoyance is by observing images and/or symbols provided by Spirit within your mind's eye. As you continue your practice, Spirit will assist you in deciphering the language of these symbols to assist you in reading for a client and gain information for yourselves.

REST IN THE KNOWINGNESS
THAT YOU HAVE 'INSIDE'.

"Find that Place of Love Within
And you will settle with ALL of Your Kin.
Find that Place of Love Beyond
And Gain further Images to help you there on.

In that Place of Love and Rest
you gain fulfillment to do all the rest.
Your life on earth does take its toll
But you have such wisdom to assist you and behold.

You must remain here with your kin,
but you can continue to find peace and contentment as you
go Within.
You will find that All is well
As you continue your devotion that serves you in the knell".

Via Gerri

Chapter Three

Knowing your Psychic Strengths

HOW WILL I KNOW MY PSYCHIC STRENGTHS?

Everyone has the four psychic centers mentioned in the previous section; however, some people may have more power or strength in one particular area.

Some of us have become aware of these gifts and some have not yet made this discovery and, of course, some are not willing or open to exploring these gifts.

As you continue your practice with a Spiritual and Psychic development circle you can begin to become aware of which Psychic center is operating at what time, which psychic strength you are most comfortable with.

One center is not better than another. It is just a matter of discovering and becoming aware of how Spirit works with you. You may also begin to notice how one center that was not particularly active is now changing and becoming stronger as you work with these gifts.

Each of us has a very different style of learning and observing what goes on around us, we are all unique. Some of us are much more **visual** and they learn by seeing or reading the information or by demonstration. Some of us prefer to use our **listening skills** and learn by listening to the subject matter, lectures, books on tape and other listening exercises. Still other students need to **feel** the work at hand through their sense of touch and learn through the use of Reiki or many of the healing arts. They are more kinesthetic.

Many of those who have trained as teachers of young children often use a variety of activities to teach the same subject in an attempt to engage all of their students. They may allow the children to observe, write or touch whatever they are in the process of learning about. These teachers honor the various styles of learning significant to each student.

In summary, the various terms of psychic strengths are:

**Those who are Psychic Feelers are called Clairsentients.
Those with Psychic Intuition are called Claircognizants.
Those with Psychic Hearing are called Clairaudients.
Those who have Psychic Visions are called Clairvoyants.**

Again, we all have these abilities but with some work and support we are all able to discover which psychic strength is most comfortable for us to work with.

Those who have strength in **Psychic intuition** come to trust their own sense of "Inner Knowing". They do not know how they know, they just know they know!!

Those who have strength in **Psychic Vision** tend to review all of their options before they can make a decision. They need to 'See' all the angles first.

Those who have strength in **Psychic Feeling** may have a tendency to become overwhelmed or drained by the energies of those people around them. Another word frequently used to describe this phenomenon is "empathic". These people may benefit by learning how to discern between their own energy and the energy belonging to others.

A simple phrase to say to help remain with our own energy is to say: **"I ask to be cleared of any energy pattern around me that does not belong to me. May I be protected and filled with Love and Light and Strength."**

Those who have strength in **Psychic Hearing** gain information from the words and phrases they hear in their mind. They may choose to make their decisions only after they have a discussion with them Selves.

DISCOVERING YOUR PERSONAL PSYCHIC STRENGTHS

As you become more aware of your particular Psychic Strength, you will come to know and better understand your means of operating in the world. You can also come to understand more fully the 'style' of those whom you both live with and work with.

Are there people in your life who just know what you are going to say?

Are there others who need to see the plan before making their decision?

Do you know people who won't try something new if it does not feel just right?

Do you know other people who need to analyze something from every angle before making any decisions?

You can perceive them all with love and compassion when you are able to understand that they may be coming from a different method, a different viewpoint, a different form of processing than you prefer.

The majority of people need to undertake some form of 'See', 'Hear', 'Know', or 'Sense' before they can be comfortable in making a choice. On the next page are several questions specific to each psychic gift. These questions are there to assist you in discovering your innate abilities.

QUESTIONS TO HELP YOU UNDERSTAND YOUR PARTICULAR PSYCHIC PERSONALITY

Clairsentience

Can you sense when someone is upset, without any words being exchanged?

Can you be feeling just fine then meet someone and suddenly find that your mood changes?

As you walk into a room, can you sense that there had been an argument before you arrived there?

Do you become somewhat confused and uncomfortable while visiting the grocery store, shopping mall or any large, crowded stores?

Claircognizance

Do you know who is phoning before you pick up the telephone?

Do you know what someone is going to say before they say it?

Do you find that you receive many ideas at once?

Do you finish other people's sentences?

Do you find yourself saying "I just know" in response to questions?

Clairaudience

Do you hear sounds in your mind, whether song lyrics or narrative that gives you inner guidance?

Do you hear music or poetry and write it down?

Do you sometimes hear words spoken out loud that have given you a warning or helped you in some way?

Can you hear more than what someone is actually telling you?

Do you find that you give an answer to a question that has not even been asked out loud yet?

Clairvoyance

Do you prefer to see the whole picture before making a decision?

Are you happier when something looks just right?

Do you like things to be picture perfect?

Are you able to see how something will work out, seeing possible solutions?

Do you visualize or imagine how something will turn out?

Chapter Four

What is a Lightworker?

The term "Lightworker" can mean different things to different people. Below I have attempted to give you an overall description of the term Lightworker.

A Lightworker is a Spiritual Being having a Human Experience as opposed to a Human Being having a Spiritual Experience.

A Lightworker has awakened or is in the process of awakening to the Re-Membrance of who they are and that they are here to help and be of service to their fellow man, animals and Mother Earth.

A Lightworker has Re-membered how to work with the energy fields that exist around all living things, people, animals, trees and nature.

A Lightworker has Re-Membered or is Re-membering their psychic abilities of Sight, Sound, Feeling and Hearing on the Spiritual Level. All Lightworkers assist each other in raising their vibratory rates and clearing themselves of all that no longer serves them.

A Lightworker has Re-Membered that we ALL are One.

A Lightworker is Re-Membering their Higher Self and is communicating with this Higher Self.

Perhaps you have identified that you are seeking to do all of these things and that you are now Re-Membering who and what you are. Perhaps you, too, are a Lightworker here to assist all.

It is important for all Lightworkers to Re-gather with each other, to continue to share what they have learned about Love and Light with each other and with the world.

Chapter Five

Creating Sacred Space

HOW CAN I CREATE A SACRED SPACE AROUND ME?

A Sacred Space can be created around you simply by placing your intention on having this take place. You can call upon all the Highest and Best healing energies as these energies are here to support you along the way.

You may call upon Divine Father and Mother, the Highest and Best Angelic vibrations as well as any of the Ascended Masters and Divine Healers.

You may also call on Mother Earth and all of her elements: the Elementals, Plants, Animals, Bodies of Water, Rocks and Mountains.

You can call upon Father Sky and all the elements that make up the sky: the Sun, the Moon, the Stars, the Planets, the Angelic Beings, Constellations, Star Beings, Galaxies and Ascended Masters.

You can call upon the 4 directions (North, South, East and West) and all the supporting energies and animal medicines that are associated with them.

You contribute to creating Sacred Space through the practice of stating your intentions, requesting help and healing. It is important to **open your sacred space** with this practice before doing any healing work. It is equally important to give thanks, honor and reverence when your healing work is complete and to **close your healing space** with this ritual.

Chapter Six

Energetic Protection

HOW DO I ENERGETICALLY PROTECT MYSELF AND MY FAMILY FROM THE DISHARMONIOUS ENERGY OF PEOPLE, PLACES AND THINGS?

Because energy follows thought, by placing your intention you create Sacred Space around you, your family and your home.

The use of incense, candles, sound, light, sage, Spiritual Pictures and Symbols can help to protect and clear any location. Learning some of these techniques for clearing your energy field, your chakras, can assist you in remaining clear. This also assists in preventing negative energies from coming in, energies that might not be at all helpful to you.

You can also use recordings of crystal and metal bowls to clear your space. These sounds are specifically designed to assist you in clearing your space. You can purchase many different CD's specifically designed to guide you through a meditation that can clear your chakras.
 (See Recommended Music page.)

With your intention, you should envision White Light around both yourself and your family members. At the same time ask Spirit to provide what is best for you and for anyone you would like to protect.

You must remember we do not exactly know what is best for anyone. We can ask, with the best of intentions, but ask without any attachments to the outcome. Calling upon the Highest and Best Guides to assist you is always a wise thing to do. Then watch for signs and see how they go to work!

Prayer for Protection

I ask for only the Highest and Best in Love, Light and Wisdom to be here present.
I thank Divine Mother and Father for being here with me.
I welcome in the Highest and best Angelic Vibrations, Ascended Masters and the Loving Presence of Father Sky and Mother Earth.

I ask that this room be filled with a sphere of the most beautiful golden-white light and that it be filled with compassion for myself and all others.

I ask that Archangel Michael surround this space with his Legion of Angels and that he escort any and all energies that are not here for my highest and best purpose back to their proper time and place for their continued progress and wellbeing.

I ask for and invite the highest and best wisdom that is important for me today.

I ask that this guidance be given to me in a clear fashion that I may fully understand.

Chapter Seven

Clearing Energy

HOW DO I CLEAR THE ENERGY IN MY LIVING SPACE?

You can clear the energy in your living space by creating A Sacred Space all around you. **Always** ask for the Highest and Best Golden White Light of protection to fill your space. Call upon your Highest and Best Guides, Ascended Masters, Angelic Beings, Teachers and Healers.

In conjunction with that, you can use **Sound** for the clearing and energy balancing of your chakras. There is a wide variety of music that is available to play to assist you with this. Some my favorites are the 'Moon Suite' or 'Seven Metals' as these allow the vibrations of the Singing Bowls to clear your home or workplace of any lower, denser vibrating energy that may be stuck in these spaces. These CD's use the vibration of crystal bowls and brass bowls to assist in dissipating lower energies making way for higher vibrations as they cleanse and clear your environment. Crystal Bowls, using bells, rattles and drums are also very effective in clearing your living space.

You can use **Fragrance** by burning incense, sage, fragrant candles and aromatherapy oils. Each of these substances offer specific fragrances and vibratory rates that shift the energy patterns so you may achieve another type of energy in your space, clearing your space to maintain a more comfortable environment.

Incense and oils can assist in dissipating any lower vibrational energy. There are several varieties of incense and oils which are used to raise the vibration of an area, dissipating lower vibrational energies, clearing and cleansing the area. Many different cultures, in all parts of the world, use incense to clear and maintain a sacred space.

Frankincense and myrrh, or sage, cedar, sweet grass, copal, lavender and rose all serve to raise the vibrational rate and create a sacred, cleared space. These are readily available. Use whichever fragrance best resonates with you.

Symbols

You may also use **Symbols** for protection and clearing your space. For example, symbols such as a cross, an ankh, a five-pointed-star are often used to clear energy. Even pictures of your Guiding Spirits, Ascended Masters and Angels provide a portal and reminder of the much higher vibrational energy of those pictured.

When clearing space, always ask that any unnecessary energies be returned to their proper time and place by Archangel Michael. He, in particular, loves to assist in this task.

You may also call upon your Guiding Spirits to assist. You can clear the **Auric Fields** that always surround you. Everyone has their own energy field surrounding them, an electro-magnetic field that is called your aura. These energy fields can be cleared; they can be set to protect you from any energy that does not serve you, through your intentions.

Always remember, Energy follows thought.

You can set your intentions as often as you'd like or you feel is necessary. Know that you are the one in charge. The more that you are able to be in alignment with your Higher Self and with The Divine Source, the more you will be in the flow of your Divine Plan.

Visualization and Protection Exercises:

Column of Light
Envision yourself encircled by a golden-white column of light. This column of Light extends from Father Sky through your body all the way down to Mother Earth.

With each inhalation and exhalation you increase the intensity as well as the diameter of your column of light. As you continue to breathe, in and out, this column of Light fills you and encircles you. It extends out to encompass your aura at least three feet around you, and then spreads out to fill your room and beyond.

As you rest within this Light you can experience the continuous flow of Life Force energy that flows within you and around you. You are connected to the Divine Creator, the Mother and the Father and thus you are completely protected. Allow this column of light to clear, cleanse and balance your chakras and aura as needed.

Shielding your Aura:
Allow yourself to become aware of the auric field that extends three feet around you. Envision this field to be an oval-shaped sphere that completely surrounds your body and your auric field.

Place your intention for this oval sphere to take the form of a transparent crystal that will allow in only the energy that is good for you and will block out any energy that does not serve you.

Your wish is to allow this crystal sphere to protect you from any and all energies that do not serve you. It is also important to request that this crystal also reflect only Love back to those that do not serve your highest good.

Chapter Eight

The Ancient Art of Feng Shui

FENG SHUI

You can use the art of Feng Shui to aid you in clearing your home. Feng shui uses the principle of chi or "flow" to provide for the best movement of energy in your home or work place. By placing furniture and other objects in strategic places it allows for the correct "flow" or chi to be present in your life.

Feng Shui originated in China approximately 4000 years, long before the Birth of Christ. The primary purpose, as above, is to allow for a balanced flow of energy in your life body and your environment. There is a direct link between the flow of energy in your environment to how smoothly things are running in your life.

Feng Shui has been shown to assist people in attracting health, wealth and wellbeing.

By learning some simple techniques involving the correct placement of objects and furniture in the rooms of your home you can enhance the flow of Chi (energy) and thus enhance your life.

The basic premise is that different areas of your life are governed by the different areas or rooms in your home or work environment.

The state of the energy around and in you can be changed and shifted by making small adjustments to your environment. Feng Shui is an art and practice that can help you on many different levels.

As you explore Feng Shui further, you may find that you have already innately utilized many of the Feng Shui principles in your home. You might notice that you feel better when you place your chairs facing the door of your room, rather than having your back to the door.

You may already have experienced the difference in your home after a good spring cleaning. These changes affect your home environment and you.

For example, the condition of your Kitchen and Bathroom relates to your wealth and prosperity. Your Living Room most often relates to Family Life. The condition of your Bedroom is usually related to your emotional health as well as your close relationships.

THE LIVING ROOM

As you look around your Living room or Family room what you observe may give you some insight into the state of your life. Our inner and outer life are quite often a reflection each other.

As you look around do you see order, balance and tranquility? Or do you see disorder and disarray. Disorder is a strong indication that things within you or your life may be out of balance.

Observe the placement of the seating in the living room. The placement of the chairs and sofa can either hinder or encourage communication. For example, two chairs positioned side by side may be hindering any face to face communication. On the other hand, chairs positioned at an angle to each other can encourage good communication.

Seating that is positioned facing an entrance door is much more desirable then having you sitting with your back to the door. When your back is at a door, you are at a disadvantage as cannot see who is coming into the room. This is what is called bad chi.

THE KITCHEN

The kitchen is very important as this is the place in which food is prepared. This is the key to allowing your family to be able to generate wealth and prosperity.

Observe your kitchen as objectively as possible. Is it neat, clean and orderly? A balanced, calm kitchen can indicate that your finances are neat, clean and orderly as well.
Are your counters filled with clutter, cupboards and drawers full and disorganized, sink full of dirty dishes? This might indicate that your finances are the same condition, very disorganized and tasks that are put off until later. If you are struggling with your finances, check out both your kitchen and bathrooms and see if they are in need of de-cluttering and/or thorough cleaning and re-organizing. This simple remedy may indeed reflect upon your financial state of affairs.

As you look closely at each room in your home, see how the environment in each these rooms reflects your life as you experience it today.

Ask yourself if your bedroom is comfortable and clear of clutter. What is the state of my emotional health and my closest relationships? As you become aware of how your surroundings reflect you and your life at the present moment, you can begin to focus your attention on the specific areas in your home that are in need some tender, loving care.

Watch and observe that when these areas are properly cared for how the corresponding areas of your life also receive tender, loving care. If your close relationships are shaky, take a look at your bedroom and make any changes that are needed.

If your health is compromised, take a look at the part of your house that aligns with the health section of the Bagua Map (See page 32 of this guidebook).

When your environment is tranquil and serene, your energy body has a chance to become balanced and calm. Your energy fields of your body are restored to their natural balance. (*See further reading on Feng Shui in the Recommended Reading Section.*)

BASIC FENG SHUI CURES

Feng Shui offers a wide variety of cures or ways in which you can remedy the flow of energy in your home and environment. These curative items may include lights, mirrors, and crystals, sounds, moving objects, electricity, water and color. These items can all assist in the correction of the flow of energy, otherwise known as Chi. Chi is the electromagnetic energy that flows throughout the entire universe and within each of us.

LIGHT

Have you ever noticed how your mood changes on a bright, sunny day as compared to a gloomy, rainy day? On a sunny day you almost always feel emotionally happier and uplifted. Sunshine has its own Chi, which affects us in many positive ways. The use of natural light is very beneficial to us.

One way to enhance the vitality of a room is to be sure it is brightly lit. To assist you in maintaining focus on the work in front of you, try adding a brightly lit desk lamp to better illuminate your task. For a more relaxed atmosphere, dimly lit lamps would be your choice. Wall lights that shine towards the ceiling will help to diffuse direct light on the lower part of the room but still add light and brightness.

MIRRORS

Mirrors are a very simple remedy to re-adjust the flow of energy or chi. Used in a room that has an irregular shape, mirrors can help to re-direct the Chi in a more positive direction. Mirrors placed in a small bathroom will give the illusion of additional space.

Mirrors can be placed near windows so they may enhance the natural lighting and bring additional Chi into a room. Mirrors placed across from a door provide a reflective surface for any energy that is brought in by the opening of the door.

CRYSTALS

Crystals have multiple uses as they both magnify and radiate energy. They store energy and provide us with numerous qualities specifically for healing purposes. Crystals can be used as remedies to enhance the Chi by placing them in front of windows as they will capture the sunlight when entering a room.

Crystals may be hung from the ceiling in the middle of a room or any place where you want to enhance the flow of energy. They are particularly useful in corners or to block any sharp angles.

Crystals have the ability to amplify and clarify spiritual communication coming through you. You may hold a crystal in your non-dominant hand when you provide psychic readings to enhance the receiving of information.

Crystals also have the ability to absorb energy so it is a good idea to clear and cleanse your crystals on a regular basis. You may place them in the sun light or moon light to become cleared. You may also rinse them in water but be careful of soaking them in salt water as this may cause erosion in some types of crystals.

SOUND

As you know, the use of sound is very helpful to clear energy and to dissipate lower vibrational frequencies that no longer serve us.

In Feng Shui, objects that create sound are used as remedies. The most common remedy is wind chimes, especially those made of metal. This is an example of a remedy that uses sound and motion to stimulate an area that needs enhancement.

Some typical applications might involve placing a wind chime in the corner of a room to stimulate the Chi. You might also place a wind chime by your front door to enhance the beneficial energy coming into your home.

MOVEMENT

Feng shui promotes the use of movement through items. These items offer assistance in moving blocked or congested energy. The movement brought in through the use of such items as wind chimes, mobiles and clocks allow these congested energies to dissipate.

LIVE PLANTS

Live, healthy plants may be placed most anywhere in a room to help the flow of energy in a room. If you wish to enhance the energy in a space it is recommended that you use plants that have angular, spiky leaves. These plants can be placed in corners to awaken the energy that might collect there.

If you are seeking to subdue and create a relaxing environment, you can use plants that have rounded leaves. These plants work well when placed in front of a corner in your wall that protrudes out into the room. This will serve to soften the energy that might radiate from that corner.

A well placed aquarium may also serve to assist with the flow of energy. Within the fish tank you are providing living items, light and movement. This provides many remedies all in one. Aquariums placed in your wealth corner serve to enhance the energy there. (see the Bagua map on page 32).

ELECTRICAL APPLIANCES

Electrical appliances are also helpful to move the energy in a room or in a particular location within a room. When you are aware of what area in your home you would like to adjust you can use these remedies to clear this blockage and/or congestion.

COLOR

As you look at the Bagua Map you can learn which color is assigned to the various directions and areas in your home or rooms or even on your desk. You can then utilize the designated color for each direction in order to enhance that section of your home.

Colors that represent fire such as red, orange, pinks and purples are used to enhance the Southern portion in your home. The Northern portion of your home is represented by the water element which is the opposite of fire. Thus it may be more beneficial to enhance this area by using colors that represent water, such as blues, blacks and grays.

WATER ELEMENTS

Objects that provide continuous movement of water, such as fountains, help to stimulate the Chi in whatever area it is placed. For example, if you are interested in financial prosperity you would place the fountain in the South-east corner of your home.

As mentioned earlier, an aquarium offers many remedial qualities for the home. You can also create a simple water movement and a light remedy by placing a floating candle in a lovely bowl of water. When using water remedies, be certain that the water stays clean. No stagnation, please. Clean water remedies can enhance the specific quality of the designated area; stagnant waters will upset the tranquility that you wish to achieve.

If you would like to enhance your relationships with a water remedy, place your remedy in the relationship corner and keep the water free from any stagnation, so the relationship will flow free and clear as well.

BAQUA MAP

Wealth & Prosperity	Fame & Reputation	Relationships, Love & Marriage
Blues, Purples & Reds	Reds/Fire	Reds, Pinks and Whites
Health & Family	Center	Creativity & Children
Blues, Greens/Wood	Yellow/Earth Tones	White, Pastels/Metal
Self-understanding & Knowledge	Career	Helpful Friends & Travel
Black, Blues and Greens	Black, Dark Tones/Water	White, Grays and Black

Chapter Nine

All about Auras

WHAT IS AN AURA?

The Auric Field is an electromagnetically charged area of receptivity and protection that is alive with Life Force Energy continually filtering through us from the Cosmic Source, Divine Father/Mother.

Auric Fields and your chakra centers receive helpful vibrational sources and filter out all that does not serve you. The Field appears, to those who can psychically 'see', as an oval-shaped area of finely diffused color and energy surrounding each person. The colors of your auric field indicate the condition of your vibrational field and your chakras.

This oval-shaped shield and field is a recording device of every thought, word, feeling and event that has occurred in your lifetime. And like the filter in a vacuum cleaner, as these energetic experiences accumulate, it can become congested or depleted from any woundings and happenings that have occurred. Thus, it is very important to cleanse, clear and balance your chakra centers and thus your auric field from any residual wounded energy and to restore your chakras to a healed state.

There are many ways to accomplish this 'house cleaning'. Here are a few suggestions:

1. Set your intentions to cleanse, clear and balance and align your chakras and auric field with ease and grace to the level that is just right for you.

2. A Practitioner of energy balancing such as Reiki, Polarity Therapy or Shamanic Healing modalities can also assist you to clear and maintain your energy field.

3. There are several Guided Meditations CDs listed in the Recommended Guided Meditations section of this book that can lead you through this process.

4. MOST IMPORTANT - *Trust your inner knowing and intuition. It will guide you to the correct person and process for you, at the right time.*

HOW DO I TAKE CARE OF MY AURA?

A guided meditation on CD or dictated by either another person or yourself can be very beneficial in setting an intention to clear your aura.

Be aware - Energy Follows Your Thoughts.

Learning about Pranic Energy and energetic clearing methods that you can practice on yourself, are beneficial for clearing your aura. Start by placing your intention for energy clearing. Use your hand as an energetic mitt to scan your auric field at each chakra along your front and back. Your hand acts as a magnetic mitt to collect whatever energy vibration that is no longer needed and then it can be 'flicked' off into a bowl of water mixed with sea salt or into an imagined violet flame.

Visualize your chakra centers as the face of a clock that is facing out from your body. To unwind any congested energy rotate your hand counter clockwise and then 'flick' that excess energy away into the sea salt water or violet flame. To re-energize a chakra rotate your hand clockwise.

Another method utilizes your intention and your breath. Stand facing the East to the Sun, whether inside or outside your home. Breathe into your root chakra all the energy of the Sun and allow it to rotate gently to cleanse, clear and balance the root chakra. See it as bright red. On the exhale, release all that no longer serves you in this chakra. Continue breathing into each successive chakra, exhaling all that no longer serves you. Envision the remaining chakra colors: orange, yellow, green, blue, indigo, white or violet and breathe these into each of the remaining chakras.

This will only take seven breaths to accomplish and you will have cleansed, cleared and balanced your chakras which will assist your aura to come to balance and harmony.

 As we come to remember that we are Spiritual Beings having a physical experience, we begin to look at ourselves in a very different way. We begin to sense that there is an importance in maintaining our Energetic and Spiritual body as well as our physical body.

Beginning to value the practice of prayer and meditation as part of our daily care routine is most beneficial.

Changing our thought patterns from those of fear to thoughts of love, kindness, gratitude, compassion for ourselves and thus for others helps us to extend this to the universe and all that lives there. As we extend our electromagnetic auric field around us, we embrace all that is. We are all connected, as One, under the Sun/Son.

It is important for us to maintain a clear, healthy, aura because our aura is directly associated with the physical systems from which they radiate.   A healthy aura helps us to support our mental, emotional bodies as well.

A well–grounded, shielded aura, protects us from any and all energies that do not serve us.

Chapter Ten

All about Chakras

WHAT ARE CHAKRAS AND HOW DO I KEEP THEM HEALTHY?

You are surrounded by your auric field and within that is housed your physical body and the energy centers called chakras. You are an energetic being composed of pure energy of light, love and intelligence. This life force energy is unlimited and fills you with amazing gifts of strength and wisdom.

Since Energy Follows Thought, your thoughts are very powerful. Your thoughts influence the flow of energy within and around you.

You become what you focus upon.

Your feelings are determined by where you are focusing your thoughts.
You attract to yourself more of what you are focusing on. As you shift your awareness from sad, depressing thoughts to happy uplifting events, you begin to feel better because you have shifted your energy vibration from a lower, denser rate of vibration to a higher, lighter rate. Thus you begin to feel lighter and happier.

By making a gratitude list naming things you are grateful for starting with the letter 'A" in the alphabet continuing through to the letter 'Z' you can practice and exercise that provides a lift for your energy field. All of these thoughts affect the specific energy centers of your body. These energy centers are called Chakras. (Shock-rahs).

Chakra is the ancient Sanskrit word for 'wheel'. These wheels of energy are found along the body and correspond to the glandular system of the body.

The Life Force energy that comes to us from The Divine Source is brought to us through these chakras providing us with Wisdom and Psychic awareness.

Chakras know what to do on their own. They continually send out and receive energy for our benefit. Sometimes we need a chakra tune-up.

As you move through your life, your chakras may collect heavy, dense energy, similar to the over-worked filter on your vacuum cleaner. The chakra may become congested and be in need of clearing so it can breathe freely and move energy more efficiently. Thus you experience the flow of energy within you to a much greater extent and experience a greater sense of well being.

As your chakras receive their energetic 'tune-up' you may find that your Spiritual and Psychic Senses become more acute. You are more able to psychically See, Hear, Sense or Know.

Each chakra addresses a particular life issue. The location of the chakras, along with corresponding to our physical body is associated with the personal issues surrounding these physical centers.

For example, the heart chakra can manifest as congested energy when you experience a loss in your life. Your throat chakra may need energizing after experiencing a period when you could not 'speak your truth'. There are ways of exploring the energetic causes of dis-ease. Sometimes, if a person is under great stress and their solar plexus, your center of will and power, feels restricted, you could develop actual physical symptoms of indigestion as the body reacts to the energetic happenings around it.

So, if we begin to shift our thoughts to thoughts of faith and love, the chakras have the opportunity to run at a healthy state. Your Life force energy can flow more smoothly creating for you an inner and outer environment of harmony and joy. When your chakras are working, are balanced and clear, you can begin to more easily observe guidance and wisdom about yourself and for others.

Energy clearing sessions such as Reiki, can be extremely helpful in clearing your chakras and energy fields of old, perhaps heavy, dense energetic debris of the past.

Such clearing allows your chakras to breathe and work more efficiently. They become aligned with ease and Grace allowing you to maintain health and happiness. This opening of your psychic centers can bring you your inner seeing, sensing, hearing and knowing.

Your chakras know just what to do to help you maintain your vibrant energy, your guiding intuition and innate abilities. All of this is within you awaiting your re-membrance of your SELF.

More Specific Information About Your Chakras:

Each chakra spins at a different rate of speed. The chakras in the upper part of your body spin at a faster rate than those in the lower part of your body.

Your root, sacral and solar plexus chakras relate to the material world with your heart chakra representing the mid-point. Your throat, third eye and crown chakras relate to the Spiritual world.

The chakras spin clockwise as they are being energized and counter-clockwise as they are being released. The lower 3 chakras rotate at slower vibrations and have the color vibrations of the warm colors; red, orange and yellow. The upper chakras, spin at a much faster rate of vibration and have radiate cool colors of green, blue, violet and purple.

As you continue to clear, cleanse and balance your chakras you will begin to open and become more able to see, hear, feel and sense information from your Higher Self and from auras. *(For further, more in-depth information about chakras, see the book Chakra Clearing by Doreen Virtue.)*

Your first major chakra is the **root chakra** which is located at the base of your spine and vibrates with the energy of the color red. The root chakra is associated with issues of survival, security and support in the physical world. It deals with your feeling of safety, of having enough and of being supported by others.

Your second major chakra is the **sacral chakra** which is located three to four inches below the navel that vibrates with the energy of the color orange. This chakra is associated with your creativity and procreativity.

Your third major chakra is the **solar plexus** located above your waistline in the area of the stomach. This chakra vibrates with the energy of the color of bright yellow and is your center of power, will and of Clairsentience.

Your fourth major chakra is the **heart chakra** which is located in your chest area. This chakra vibrates with the energy of the color emerald green or pink. It represents your center of love, forgiveness and relationships.

Your fifth major chakra is the **throat chakra** which is located at your throat and vibrates with the energy of a light blue color. This is your center of communication, speaking your truth and asking for what you need.

Your sixth and seventh chakras **(ears)** are located inside your head just above your physical ears. These chakras vibrate with the energy of the color of red-violet. This is your center of Divine Communication and is where you hear and experience Clairaudience.

The eighth major chakra is the **brow chakra** located between your eyes on your forehead. This chakra vibrates with the energy of the color indigo blue. This is the center of your Psychic Sight into the past and future, your Clairvoyance.

The ninth major chakra is the **crown chakra** and is located inside the top of your head and vibrates with the energy of the color purple. This is your center for receiving Divine Guidance and your Claircognizance.

CLEARING THE CHAKRAS

Clearing can be accomplished through meditation and visualization. Chakra clearing involves the clearing and balancing of your chakras.
You will want to clear yourself, with the use of higher vibrational energies, anything that no longer serves you.
 You also want to balance the size of the chakras so that they all rotate and spin at the same rate.

The Use of Color to Calm or Activate Chakras

We can envision colors to assist in clearing and cleansing our chakra systems and also to provide the energy from these colors to calm or activate the chakras.

Here is a suggested list of colors:

Root Chakra - use red to activate and green to calm.
Sacral Chakra - use orange to activate and blue to calm.
Solar Plexus Chakra - use yellow to activate and violet to calm.
Heart Chakra - use green to activate and pink, soft red to calm.
Throat Chakra - use sky blue to activate and orange to calm.

Brow Chakra - use indigo to activate and soft orange/pink to calm.
Crown Chakra - use violet to activate and yellow to calm.

BASIC MEDITATION GUIDANCE:

Your own INNER GUIDANCE (gut feeling) is the most important source of instruction in meditating– *or doing anything,* for that matter. Pay attention to your own body wisdom and you will be following your Highest Guidance.

First, sit comfortably in a quiet place where you can be alone without interruption.

Next, sit in whatever position that feels most comfortable for you.

Then, close your eyes and begin to breathe gently at your own pace. Take two or three full, deep breaths, breathing in the healing life force energy and exhaling all that no longer serves you. Relax - just breathe and relax.

As you begin to meditate, just observe any thoughts that might appear. Try to avoid latching onto them or fighting with them - just notice the thoughts and/or feelings and allow them to just pass on through. For example, you can visualize a fearful thought and place it in a bubble and then watch as it just floats away.
 You can also use your breath to assist you to exhale the fearful thoughts and to breathe in Love and Light.

In the following pages are some sample meditations that you may practice. You may either read these out loud or record them for your own personal use. Once you feel centered in a comfortable position just follow along with the meditation. If you choose, you may purchase the CD of this meditation, "Seeds of Awakening", available at www.findpeacewithin.com

or any other meditation CD that speaks to you and will assist you as you seek to achieve a balanced state.

Meditation – Clearing the Chakra Centers

The maintenance of the seven chakras, the energy centers, is extremely important in the development of your psychic abilities and physical, emotional and spiritual health. Chakras are constantly spinning vortices of energy and may become congested due to overuse and can affect us on many levels. Chakra clearing meditations and/or hands-on-healing sessions such as Reiki, Polarity Therapy and Shamanic modalities can be very beneficial to the tuning up of your energy body.

Mother Earth Meditation – Clearing from your Root Chakra to the Crown Chakra

This meditation can be found on the "Seeds of Awakening" CD by Gerri Shanti DeSimone, M.Ed.

"And now, asking for only the highest and best for ourselves and each other, allow yourself to breath, to breathe in the life force energy from Mother Earth, inhaling her healing energy, exhaling what no longer serves you.

And maintaining your awareness of your connection to Mother Earth, start your journey upward, slowly carrying the life force energy that exudes throughout your body, given freely from Mother Earth.

And placing your intention to allow your chakras to be aligned with ease and grace, observe as it slowly rises into your feet, through the soles of your feet. Allow it to rise gently along your legs, to your knees, along you thighs, into your hip area, then to the base of your spine where the energy will cleanse, clear and balance the first chakra, your center of security in the world.

Allow the energy of this ruby red light to encircle this center and allow its red energy frequency to rotate and clear this chakra of any and all unwanted energy. And inhale what you need and gently exhale what no longer serves you.

And next allow this beautiful flowing energy to gather amidst your second chakra, your sacral chakra, the center of your creativity and pro-creativity. See here the energy of a vibrant, orange glowing light, cleansing, clearing and balancing this chakra of any and all unwanted, unnecessary energy. Feel the gentle spinning motion as this chakra is cleared and balanced. And allow your gentle inhale to enhance the vibration of the orange light and allow your exhale to release all that no longer serves you here.

And now allow the loving Mother Earth energy to flow along up to your third chakra, your solar plexus, the center of your will and strength. See here the energy of a brilliant yellow light, cleansing, clearing and balancing this chakra, this center of power. Allow any and all unwanted energy to be cleansed and cleared from this center, utilizing your breath to inhale the healing energy and to exhale any unwanted, unneeded energy.

And now, as you inhale allow this energy to move up to your, fourth chakra, your heart center, visualizing the healing energy of green light, gently spinning, cleansing, and clearing your heart center, your center of compassion for yourself and for others. Feel the pulsing movement of energy in your heart center as it gently clears any unwanted, unneeded energy allowing you to feel open and relaxed. Again, inhale what you want and exhale what you no longer need.

And now, using your breath, allow this healing energy to move along into your fifth chakra, your throat chakra, your center of speaking your truth, of creating with your voice.

See here the energy of a pale blue colored light, cleansing and clearing this center, as it becomes balanced, you can feel its gentle pulse, clearing away all blockages to your free speech. Breathe in this beautiful blue energy and exhale all that no longer serves you here.

Now as the energy moves into your sixth chakra, your third-eye center, you observe the energy of a lovely indigo blue light rotating gently to cleanse and clear your center of Psychic Sight, your place of visual wonders in the world and of The World Beyond. Allow this center to be cleared of any and all obstructions to Psychic Sight, experiencing the gentle pulse of light energy here. And as you inhale, allow the indigo light to intensify as it clears this center and as you exhale, allow any energy that does not serve you to move gently back to Mother Earth for transmutation, to be restored to healing energy once again.

And now you are at your seventh chakra, your crown center, your center of Wisdom, of connecting with the Divine, the Place in which the life force energy enters your body from above. See here the energy of a beautiful white light, perhaps white golden light, allow it to cleanse clear and balance this center, allow this area to be freed of any and all energies that no longer serve you. Feel the gentle flow of energy as it clears and strengthens your connection to Source, your Connection with The Divine. Gently inhale what you need and exhale what no longer serves you.

Now that you have cleansed and cleared your chakra system allow yourself to bask in the beautiful energy of Source that flows within you there, the energy that flows through you from Father Sky and from Mother Earth.

Allow these energies to intermingle within you there, a continuous flow of energy, always loving and supporting you here. Visualize the red energy of Mother Earth, intermingling with the white energy coming through your crown from Father Sky. See a sweet, gentle pink energy vibration filling your being, spreading out through your aura, intensifying as it spreads out to those around you and to the world.

You are a Beacon of Light, of Loving Light, shining now for all the World to see, to see their worth, to see their strength, to see themselves as a reflection of the God Source Within them there. May your chakras be aligned with ease and Grace, and be opened to the level that you need as you go forward into your day.

Slowly now, begin your journey back to the present moment, taking a nice deep breath, beginning to move fingers and toes, feeling yourself upon your chair, knowing that you can return to this state whenever you want to, remembering your journey, feeling refreshed and relaxed. When you are ready, open your eyes and drink some water.

And if you choose, continue to experience this Loving Flow of Energy, through you there for as long as you wish."

This meditation can be found on the "Seeds of Awakening" CD by Gerri Shanti DeSimone, M.Ed.

Father Sky Meditation – Clearing from your Crown Chakra to your Root Chakra

This meditation can be found on the *"Seeds of Awakening" CD by Gerri Shanti DeSimone, M.Ed.*

"And now asking for only the highest and best for ourselves and each other, as you are resting here, allow yourself to become aware of your breath, breathing in and out, inhaling life force energy and exhaling all that no longer serves you.

Breathing now at your own pace, full and deep, relaxed and easy, just breathe. Bring yourself to that centered place within, to that comfortable place of relaxation. And as you begin to relax, bring your attention to the top of your head and at this place bring downward the whitest light shining through your being and allow it to flow, ever so slowly, through you there and allow it to bring you peace and quiet and happiness. Allow this Light to make its way down through your **crown** and there to receive any and all information that is needed at this time and to become aware of the cleansing of this chakra.

As this Light moves down throughout the crown you can begin to see with New Eyes for your **third eye center** is the next to be cleared. Allow this Light to cleanse and clear your third eye and 'See' with New Eyes, 'Know' with a clearer knowing, for these are the places of your re-birthing. As this Light moves on down through the crown and third eye, it clears the way for the passage of your youth, for the time when you seek to Say your Words for All to hear.

So allow this Light to cleanse and clear your **throat** center bringing in clarity and precision of truth for your voice and deeds and then allowing this Light to traverse through the crown, third eye and throat. You are opening up to the possibility that your **heart center** can now be cleared and cleansed. The heart center is the place where most sorrow is held and it is here that This Light can cleanse, clear and balance your heart center. For it is here that more shall be felt and given to thee and those around you there.

Allow this Light to gently swirl in its attempt to clear and cleanse. Your heart center is now clear and balanced allowing you to continue downward to the **solar plexus**. For it is here that your will is expressed and repressed. Allow the Light to gently cleanse and clear your solar plexus bringing you freedom from contempt of others and yourself. For it is here that your will gets tampered with and it is here that you begin **to see** your truth and **speak** your truth and **love** yourself in this action.

And now as the Light continues its journey through the upper chakras, allow this light to settle within your **sacral area**. For it is here that so much pain and discomfort has been expressed. Allow this Light to cleanse, clear and balance this part of your being. Allow yourself to be cleansed and balanced inside and out as this Light flows downward once more to **the base of your spine**, to your root, your place of basic trust and nourishment.

For it is here that you connect with Mother Earth. It is here that you find your grounding and foundation. Allow this area to be cleansed and balanced and healed, as well, providing you with a sturdy, safe support system.

And as this Light continues to flow down to Mother Earth, you will also feel the upward motion of this Light reaching for the Father, the Divine Father, that shines down on us from Above.

For it is here that you make your connection with the Divine, and traverse this energy connected to Mother Earth. As this flow of energy continues to expand, feel yourself lighter and lighter, yet grounded in stability, balanced in Love with the Father and the Mother, Father Sky and Mother Earth.

Give a glance at the wondrous aspects of your Self, that Self that is hidden away but now remains to Be 'Seen'. Allow yourself to experience this flow of Light Energy. Allow it to balance you, to cleanse you and to heal your Being.

Remain here for awhile, for as long as you like, connected in love to the Father and the Mother. And when it's time to return, begin by taking a nice, deep, cleansing breath, gently moving fingers and toes, knowing that you can remember this journey and return to this place whenever you would like, feeling refreshed and re-newed.

And when you are ready, slowly come back to this time and place by opening your eyes and then drinking some water.

***This Mediation can be found on the** " Seeds of Awakening " Cd by Gerri Shanti DeSimone, M.Ed.*

Reminders:

Placing your intention to have your chakras cleansed, cleared and balanced is all you need.

Energy Follows Thought.

Divinely Originated Thoughts (D.O.T.), are always presented in positive terms. Do not follow negative guidance because that may be from your lower ego self and not Divine Guidance. Trust your Intuition, your gut feelings. Just keep 'Following the DOTS'.

Here are some other Methods that can open, clear, align and balance your chakras:

Using toning, chanting, exercise, yoga poses, flower essences, aromatherapy, crystals, food and diet.

Keeping your chakras, cleared and balanced will help you to enjoy the never-ending life force energy and clear, focused intuition held by your Higher Self.

When you feel upset and down for no apparent reason,
CLEAR AND BALANCE YOUR CHAKRA CENTERS

If you need clear insight and information,
CLEAR AND BALANCE YOUR CHAKRAS

Chapter Eleven

Spirit Seeks our Attention

In this chapter we will discuss the many **SIGHTS AND SOUNDS OF SPIRIT COMMUNICATION.**
We will also discover some of the many ways that **SPIRIT TRIES TO GET OUR ATTENTION.**

Spirit is continually trying to gain our attention, trying to assist us on our journey with the many Sight and Sounds around us. The songs of the birds, the numbers on digital clocks, the lyrics from the songs on the radio all signal that we are not alone, that we are loved and all connected as One.

The Divine Source in Its All - Knowing Spiritual Intelligence has provided us with moments of awe and wonder at the supposed synchronicities around us. When we pay attention to the continual Sights and Sounds of the Holy Spirit, it connects with us again and again, providing us with Sights, Sounds, Symbols and Messages of support and love.

The more we pay attention to the Sights and Sounds presented to us by Spirit, the more validation and encouragement is sent to us in this fashion.
As you begin this journey of paying attention to the Language of Spirit, the Sights and Sounds of Spirit, your life will never be the same. You will begin to see and sense the power of Spirit in your life and in the lives of those around you.

You will come to an experiential understanding that you have your own Inner Knowing, Inner Healer, and Inner Guidance all available to assist you as you Re-Member who you are and why you are here.

The Sights and Sounds of Spirit bring us affirmation that we are never alone and that we have helpers as we follow our Soul's desire and a Higher Purpose for our lives. We come to realize that earth is a school and that we do, and will, have all that we need as we Re-Member to Find Peace Within - as we go within to find our peace and joy awaiting there.

Affirmation:
"I am open to receiving the Sights and Sounds of Spirit into my life. I ask to be shown clear indications that I can easily understand".

The Sights and Sounds can be **Messages** of important information for you or they can indicate a **Reflection** of where you are or what is going on in your life.

Sights and Sounds as Messages can bring to you validation and guidance. They can be subtle and gentle reminders to assist you in remembering that you are not alone and that there are many "helpers" around to assist you to maintain balance and peace in your life.

Sights and Sounds as Reflections of your inner state of being help you to see more clearly what needs to change in your life. For example, a cluttered home could be a reflection that your mind is cluttered as well.

Sights and Sounds are a Reflection of what is Within you. The things that you notice around you are related to your Inner consciousness. The Sights and Sounds around you are a reflection of what is within you.

Why is this?

Since your thoughts are determined by your beliefs, sights and sounds that are personal to you will come from those beliefs and are influential in the creation of happenings and/or events in your life. Our conscious and subconscious beliefs can affect our lives. They become the old operating system from which we draw our awareness.   Many times we are not even aware that our subconscious is at work and quite possibly getting in our way.

Sights and Sounds Mirror Your Intentions/Attentions. The things that you are aware of in the world around you may be objects and/or situations that you are placing your concerted focus upon. For example, when you are trying to decide between purchasing two models of a new car, you may begin to see those two brands on the highway more than any other time. You have brought your attention to these two cars and the Universe presents to you what you are focusing on.

Sights and Sounds Can Bring Future Information. Sights and Sounds can bring messages from the future because of the interaction between the time-space continuum as explained by Albert Einstein. The relationship between what we know as time is inter-related with space. The measure of space in height, width and length, including the aspect of time, allows this all to loop upon itself thus maintaining the awareness of all time blended together.

Many ancient predictions have been made possible because of this interaction between time and space. The foretelling of the future from dreams, as well, is an example of this phenomenon. Pay close attention to any sign possibly from your future and write it down, as it is, perhaps, preparing you for some future event and/or reason.

Sights and Sounds originate from the collective unconscious. This is made up of the personal unconscious mind and the collective unconscious mind. These two places are your own personal "warehouse storage" for all memories of experiences that have occurred for each individual, for the entire human race.

Thus, a Sight or Sound that has been held in the collective unconscious may show up for you in order to bring you some valuable piece of information.   For example, the sight of a star may jog your unconscious memory and bring to you information that is related to the unconscious of the whole collective. The star may be a sign of protection, of our connection with the stars in the sky, our patriotic values, whatever meaning that this may hold for you. The sight of star may bring to you validation of some thought that you have recently been thinking, something that 'solidifies' at the same time when you just happen to 'observe' the star. The sign of a star, like so many other sights, may be just one of the universal sights and sounds that connect us all within the collective unconscious. Your own Higher Self and/or guides may also be sending you this image in an effort to bring you valuable information or validation.

Sights and Sounds from your Ancestral Heritage. A sight or sound that you later find out has some important significant meaning to your ancestors may show up for you. For example, perhaps you have felt it was important to wear an 'Italian Horn' on a necklace. You later find out that this has been a symbol of protection from 'The Evil Eye' in your Italian ancestry. You might not have realized or known this on conscious level but somehow you have connected into the collective unconscious of your Italian heritage.

The Sights and Sounds from nature speak to you more than many may consciously realize. Bringing yourself outside to experience nature all around you can bring to you a multitude of sights and sounds from the Animal Kingdom.

In Native American culture, they describe the 'Medicine' that each element of nature and various animals represent. Perhaps you do not consciously realize that you have a Power Animal and/or Energy Spirit with you to guide and protect you, but you do discover that for some unknown reason, you collect representations of owls, for example.

You like to place these various statues and pictures in your environment. Later, you discover that the Owl is one of your Power Animals. Its 'Medicine' is derived from the actions and nature of this animal particularly in its ability to see and hear clearly. The owl is a wonderful totem (another word for power animal) for a Spiritual Medium and Psychic as the owl has the ability to see in the dark.

(For further information on Power Animal I recommend a wonderful reference in the book "Animal Speak" by Ted Andrews)

The Sights and Sounds possibly originated from a Past Life. Since all of your experiences, from all of your lives, are recorded in your subconscious, (these are sometimes called your 'Akashic Records' or 'Auric Records') you may find that Spirit can use these memories to assist you, to warn you, or to give you validation when it is needed. You may also find that Past Life Regression therapy sessions or Auric Record Clearing Sessions (please see www.findpeacewithin.com for more information on Auric Record Clearing Sessions) can help heal old memories or past injuries and/or woundings as well.

For example, perhaps you have a very unusual fear of the water. On a conscious level you know there is no need to fear the water, but on a very visceral level you are truly terrified. Perhaps by recalling a past life in which there was a problem regarding water, you can be relieved of this fear of water in the present time. Another example would be that perhaps in a past life you valued the Sun in a most Divine way – many cultures worshipped the sun - and you find that now when you see the Sun you feel relaxed, happy and supported.

Sights and Sounds can come to us through our mechanical devices but can originate from Our Higher Self, from our Guides, Angels and Spirits. Have you begun to realize that your awareness or attention is brought to a digital clock or other device that has numbers on it? You are not specifically looking to see what time it is, you just feel that it is important to look at the clock? Sometimes you do not even register what time it is, but more so on the times that you do, you are more apt to notice that the numbers are lined up as '3:33' or '2:22'or '11:11'.

Once you begin to See, really 'See', these number, then Spirit knows it can gain your attention and give you information through the numerical meaning of numbers.

Further on in this book you will see three sections that describe the energetic meaning of numbers. Once you have developed your vocabulary on numbers and their meanings, you can begin to understand the possibilities behind what is being said to you through the acknowledgement of these various numbers. Once again, try to recall just what you were focused on or thinking about before you saw the numbers. Perhaps these numbers have shown up to give to you some type of validation, some kind of encouragement, a sign of love and some type of knowledge that you are never alone.

Radios, along with providing digital numbers also provide sound in the form or music and/or lyrics. Many people have discovered that they just happened to turn on the radio when a particularly important set of lyrics are playing, or they hear a favorite song that brings back memories of a certain person, time or place. These lyrics may remind them of a loved one or bring to them words of wisdom just at the right moment in time.

Try to remember, to recall, your most recent thoughts the next time you see or hear a particular sight and/or sound that has some meaning to you. This sight or sound may be the answer or the confirmation that you are seeking for validation at that moment.

I feel that the Sights and Sounds of Spirit are Divine Moments, Moments of Serendipity to Gain our Attention, to Show us we are not alone, that we are supported in Love.
Divine Signs are <u>real</u> - The Sights and Sounds are Divine Ways in which Spirit may manifest to all of us. You can sense, within your being, whether the sight and sound is from a divinely originated place or from another source.

Trust your inner sense, your inner knowing. Your body has a wisdom all of its own that can direct and guide you. How does the particular sight and sound feel? Does it feel warm, comfortable and loving? If not, then **always** remember that you are in control. If there is any discomfort at all you can **always** state "All that does not pertain to me and that is not in the Love and Light of God, please be returned to its proper time and place. I ask that I be filled with God's Love, Light and Strength."

DIVINELY ORIGINATED SIGNS APPEAR TO US IN MANY WAYS. They can appear through some of the many sights and sounds we have described. They can appear through our senses, our intuition, our dreams, from our collective unconscious, our culture and heritage, from Native American culture. They can come from childhood memories, past life memories and simple observations from around us through our daily lives.

The following is an example of the use of our sense of smell in receiving Spiritually Guided Messages. This is called Clairgustance:

I have a very dear friend who receives various signs from Spirit through the sense of smell and/or fragrances. She had received the fragrance of a turkey dinner at approximately the same time she discovered that a friend's mother had passed away.

As a result of this incident, when she received this same fragrance again, she realized that she had been thinking of me and simply 'Knew' that my mom had passed. Shortly after, she discovered that, in fact, this fragrance had appeared just at the same time that my mom had passed.

Spirit works in many wonder-filled ways with signs that can manifest in many ways.

There are many ways in which Spirit can gain our attention, especially once we have become aware that these sights and sounds exist.

1. **Through other people:** Notice the times when people arrive and/or leave in your life and you will find that you have gained some insight from them, perhaps learned some lesson.

2. **Through the words that are spoken:** Notice the words that you and other people use on a daily basis. For example, someone who uses the expression "I see" on a regular basis could mean that they (or you) are very visual. The term "I hear" may indicate that you or they are more audient. "I know" could mean that you or they are more cognizant. "I feel" may indicate that you or they are more able to sense.

3. **Through your thoughts:** Try to pay attention and notice the seemingly random thoughts that you might have. For example, you happen to think of an old friend and then suddenly the phone rings and it is your old friend. Notice when you make judgments of others. Quite often, this is a sign for you regarding something that you need to work on. For example saying, I think that person is too fussy over details, could be a mirror meant to show you how fussy you are over details!

4. **Through your feelings:** Notice how you feel when you talk with someone. Are you sensing their feelings or your own? Notice how you feel when you are making a decision. Does your "gut" feeling help lead you one way or another?

5. **Through your vision or hearing:** Sometimes a slip of the tongue or quick glance at something that is not what you thought it was may lead you to another thought that gives you further valuable information.

6. **Through the songs you sing or hear:** Notice what songs you might be singing to yourself. The words may be a comfort or validation for you. Songs on TV, movies, radio may also be signs of validation or a re-memberance of someone in your life, giving you the knowing that you are not alone.

7. **Through your dreams:** Notice and maybe start recording your dreams. They may contain valuable sights and sounds meant to assist you as you process old and new information about you and your life.

8. **Through printed words:** Notice words that might continually appear in your life. They may be bringing you valuable messages.

9. **Through the sights and sounds of animals and nature around you:** Notice when animals appear directly in front of you or in your dreams or meditations. They may be bringing a message that relates to their natures and/or medicine. For example, you might see an owl and be reminded of your ability to 'see in the dark' or to 'see' something beyond this reality. *(More information can be found in the book "Animal Speak" mentioned earlier).*

Feng Shui Methods of Communication

Your home environment can also be significant as a way for your higher self and/or guide to communicate with you. Pay attention and notice the Feng Shui conditions in your home. Simple things such as **Water** may represent our emotions and feelings. The state of the plumbing in your home can be a sign of your emotional state. Maintaining and keeping your plumbing fixtures free-flowing assists in allowing for healthy emotional outlets. It is important to keep your plumbing fixtures from leaking as this can indicate an overflow of emotions and/or a loss of financial resources.

Electricity can also be a sign related to your life force or your personal energy field. Keeping circuits from over-loading can bring benefits to you in maintaining a more stress-free life.

The floors and foundation in your home can be a sign of your feeling of support in this world. Take notice of your basement and its condition as it relates to your inner world.

As previously mentioned in the Feng Shui section, your home environment and the conditions present can be a reflection for you of your inner conditions, your feelings of security and support.

Even more sights and sounds......

Accidents or illness in your body: Notice your body and how it feels. Pay attention to its "whispers" so your body is not forced to shout out in pain. Observe yourself with love and understanding, with no blame, but with a watchful and willing acceptance of any possible lessons your body is showing regarding changes you might need to make.

So-called coincidences or mistakes: Notice the hidden occurrences behind every coincidence and mistake. Perhaps what we think is a mistake is a blessing in disguise. It is those sweet moments when we actually observe a coincidence that is not so coincidental!

Synchronicity: Notice those moments that are so meaningful but seem too impossible to be real. Watch for those times when you think of someone and then they just seem to appear again in your life or give you a call.

Our pets: Many of you notice how your pets communicate with you. Watch how they can in their own unique way tell you that they need food.
You have all heard of pets saving their owner from dangerous situations such as fires by giving them some type of warning signal. Pets can reflect for their owner whatever is going on for them in their environment or in their body. Pets are very psychic and quite often they sense energy shifts before we do.

Chapter Twelve

Numerology

WHY DO I KEEP SEEING DOUBLE AND TRIPLE NUMBERS?

A SPIRITUAL MESSAGE ABOUT THE ENERGY OF NUMBERS:

"Begin with the numbers. Allow them to understand the importance of these images. Numbers are signals of energy patterns that are transcribed by your central nervous system. They are underscored by the reminders that have been placed there. When you see a number you immediately re-call to yourself that part of you that you placed on the "forgotten" list. When that piece has been returned than another and another can follow through.

To see the numbers is a signal to you that ALL is WELL and in that awareness you can relax into the Knowingness of ALL that is around you there.

Follow the dots, as you say, seek the wisdom in the Actions that give you enlightenment, that lighten your load, that bring forth to you a beacon to shine the Way for you there."
Channeled via Gerri Shanti DeSimone

THE ENERGETIC MEANING OF NUMBERS

Below is a brief description behind the meanings of a few numbers (excerpt from "Healing with the Angels" by Doreen Virtue):

111- Monitor your thoughts, be sure to only think about what you want, not what you don't want.

222 - Newly planted ideas are beginning to grow into reality.

333 - Ascended Masters are near you to help, love and be companions, call upon them. For example, Jesus, Mary, Buddha, Quan Yin, etc.

444 - The angels are surrounding you, reassuring you of their love and help.

555 - Major life changes upon you, continue seeing yourself at peace.

666 - Thoughts out of balance, focused too much on the material world, balance your thoughts between heaven and earth.

777 - Angels applaud you, your wish is coming true, expect miracles.

888 - A phase of your life is about to end, there is light at the end of the tunnel. Don't procrastinate making your moves or enjoying the fruits of your labor.

999 - Completion. Message to Lightworkers- Get to work because Mother Earth needs your help right now.

000 - A reminder you are One with God and to feel the presence of your Creator's Love within you. The situation has come full circle.

*Below is a brief description behind the meanings of a few numbers (*excerpt from "Sacred Space" by Denise Linn (pages 146-153 Linn):*

11- Good for developing intuition, clairvoyance and spiritual healing

22- Unlimited potential mind, body and spirit

33- All things are possible

1- Independence, new beginnings, progress, creativity, oneness with life

2- Balance of yin and yang, self-surrender, dynamic attraction one to another before putting others before yourself

3- Communication, expression, expansion

4- Security, four elements, four sacred directions, wholeness, unity, self-discipline through work

5- Feeling free, active, vibrant, alive, ever-changing

6- Self- harmony, compassion, love arts, caring, balance

7- Inner life, mystical # symbolizes wisdom, seven chakras, birth and rebirth

8- Infinity, material prosperity, abundance, leadership

9- Humanitarian, selflessness, dedicating life to others, number of completion and of ending, release, universal compassion, tolerance and wisdom

"Triple numbers are God speaking to us."
by Drunvalo Melchizedek

The way we would interpret the numbers for ourselves has to do with whatever we are thinking or doing, or the nature of our circumstances, at the time that the number appears. Sometimes we will then have to use our intuition and/or wait to see other triple numbers for further information.

For example, if we were thinking of starting a new business and we saw triple ones, this might indicate that there was a lot of energy available for that endeavor.

The power of triple numbers comes not only from the harmonics of the moment itself, but also from the fact that it is sourced in the outside reality and therefore is not affected by our ego.

Below is what the nine possibilities mean:

111 — Energy flow- may involve money, sexual energy, movement of energy from one place to another. If we are thinking about something that is important to us when we see triple ones, this indicates that the energy is moving or being gathered in relation to that subject.

222 — this means the beginning of a new cycle. We do not know the nature of the cycle until the next triple number shows up.

333 — we are being faced with a decision. Triple threes may also mean that there may be a lesson here. Depending on your decision, it will move to 666 or 999. If you see 666 next, this signifies that the lesson will be given to you again, either

in the same manner or in some other way. When it moves to 999, then this lesson has been completed.

444 — Triple fours indicate some kind of study usually related to metaphysics or a "Mystery School". Depending upon what is happening in your life; events may be presenting us with these Mystery School lessons and information.

555 — this is the number of Christ Consciousness. It means that we have mastered a lesson in Life on our spiritual path and are now living it.

666 — we tend to think of 666 as evil, but it usually is not, except in extreme cases. Actually, it is the number of the human being, and it means density — the physical plane. Carbon, which is what organic life is based upon, has six protons, six neutrons and six electrons. In divine terms, triple sixes ask us to pay attention, to be aware, slow down and look around. If we see more than one instance of 666, we might want to consider being very careful.

777 — this is similar to 444, except it is a higher level of the Mystery School. Instead of studying, we are practicing, even playing. We are making our knowledge real in the world.

888 — Triple eights means that we have completed something in the Mystery School, whether we were at the four level or the seven level, we have mastered something.

999 — this means completion on all levels.

000 — this is the void and does not relate to this world. It is the pause between the notes of music.

Chapter Thirteen

Helping Your Children

How Can I Help My Children?
By Rebecca Kohlhorst

Do your children wake up at night or have difficulty staying in their beds?

Are they easily distracted, do they have difficulty focusing at school?

Are they uncomfortable in restaurants, malls, grocery store? (Sometimes children will show they are uncomfortable by acting out)

Do your children know when something is going to happen before it happens?

Do they seem to intuitively know they should not be around someone?

Do they say things that are beyond their years?

These are some of the things you may be noticing about your child or children, or any child in your life.

Children can be affected by the energy of others. This energy can be very disconcerting and distracting. School children are in close contact with others and different situations for the majority of their day. It can be very difficult for them to sit and focus on either the teacher or the task.

The following are some things that I have found to be very helpful and worth trying:

Teaching them to meditate.

Meditation helps all of us to focus and to feel our center, our inner power. It allows us an opportunity to quiet the noise in our mind and "settle" down.

Start with just a few minutes, especially when dealing with young children.
Play some soothing music, pick a quiet, 'special' place, sit on comfy pillows. Put in an effort to really make it a special time as meditation should be relaxing and enjoyable. If you drive your child to school you could try having your child meditate for a few minutes on the car ride to school.   Sometimes just having a few minutes of quiet focus before school can help children to be centered and more relaxed about facing their day.

Children are naturally curious. Below are several examples of conversations and exercises you could have with your child to assist them in handling their energy.

Teaching them about their Aura

Teach them how to feel their aura and how to draw it in closer and expand it out further. This helps them to not only feel their energy field but to learn how to draw it in when needed so they are not absorbing everyone else's energy.

Teaching them how to clear their Aura

Just as they brush their teeth and wash their bodies, their energy field also needs to be cleaned.

Teaching them to turn off empathy and protect themselves

This will help your children to recognize their feelings and the feelings of others. It will help them to not absorb everyone's emotions, thoughts etc.

Helping them to stay grounded

We are Spiritual Beings living in a human body. Help them to be well grounded in their bodies.

1. Teach them to bring their awareness to their feet, notice them touching the ground.
2. Suggest they imagine growing roots from their feet, connecting them to Mother Earth.
3. Connect with the earth and nature by gardening, walking in the woods, fields, parks, etc.
4. Building and making things from nature, such as Faerie Houses, bird houses made from gourds. Making teepees from vines etc. Digging in the earth is very grounding especially for children.

Providing activities that can assist your child to connect their minds and bodies.

Activities that provide movement can help when you feel that your child is not fully in their body or if they are having difficulty focusing. Eurhythmy, Tai Chi, Ballet, Fencing, Dancing, Yoga, are only a few examples. Help your child become involved in whatever activity that connects their mind and body. Watch and see how this helps them to be more calm, centered and focused.

Trusting your own inner knowing.

The most important thing that you can do to truly help your children is to be true to yourself. Trust that you know who you truly are, accepting yourself and following your path.

Your passions will teach your children to accept and love themselves. Nurture your own spiritual awakening and allow your children to watch you expand. They will learn from your experiences and your wisdom as you will learn from theirs. Children have always been my greatest teachers - you will be amazed at what they can teach you.

Stand in your Light and they will stand in theirs.

Speak with your child and, more importantly, really listen. Do not force or make them fearful. Help them to be discerning about who this information is shared with. Do not hide, but use discernment.
Teach them various protection methods. Teach them that they have choices. Teach them to live from their hearts, from the sacred place of love. Explain to them how their egos and the egos of others can deceive them, confuse them and make them fearful.

Love is always the answer.

Teach and show them by practicing meditation, by simply being still so that one may quiet down and simply hear. Teach them to keep healthy, in all the ways of their being– the physical, the emotional, the mental and the spiritual.

The foods they eat have energy. Help them to be aware of the types of foods they put in their bodies. Healthy foods can heavily influence their energy and the energy they put out.

Show them how it can help to experience nature. Teach them to experience oneness with all that is. By nurturing Mother Earth they learn the rhythms, the cycles, the "aliveness" of the Earth. Teach them to see nature and animals as nature's 'helpers'. There is so many benefits in helping them to see and experience the Magic of Nature.

Teaching them about their imagination.

Children are naturally intuitive. Intuition comes from our imagination. Imagination is what allows us to think and to communicate. Many of us have been taught that our imagination is not real, it is only make believe. Thus we are taught at an early age to leave this 'nonsense' behind in order to live in the 'real' world.

Spirit, Divine Inspiration and Intuition come to us, just as simple thoughts and communications, through our imagination. We see an apple in our minds and we communicate apple. Spirits communicate with us in the same way.

As adults, many of us are re-discovering what was once already there. Imagination is the key and children already hold this key. Offering support and interest in our children's intuitions and imagination will help them to stay open.

Allowing and encouraging them to keep their imagination.

Most of what happens when adults decide to allow Spirit to come in is the re-discovering of what was already there. What you sealed up under lock and key now needs to be re-discovered and released. How much easier it would be if humans did not have to unlearn so much, so profoundly. Imagination is key.

Creating a calm, centered, nurturing creative, loving and accepting environment is most important for all.

Create an environment that allows them to connect with their spirituality. Create a bedroom that is a sanctuary, a bedroom that allows them to truly rest and relax. This is a very important space that will allow them to get away from the outside world and feel secure and rejuvenated.

Some suggested reading:

"The Indigo Children" by Lee Carroll

"The Care and Feeding of Indigo Children" by Doreen Virtue.

Chapter Fourteen

Toys and Tools

Below are a variety of methods meant for you to have fun and play. Spirit may guide us in any number of ways so play with a few that may appeal to you. The important thing to remember is to relax and don't put pressure on yourself.

Asking for a Helpful Sight or Sound

Sometimes when we need help with decisions or specific questions, we feel the need to call for help. This is when a Sight or Sound may be useful, especially when we cannot hear or see what the Universe is sending to us.

A few Methods for asking for a sign:

Tossing a coin or using a pendulum or asking to see a specific Sight or Sound to indicate a yes or no answer.

First, clear your mind and completely let go. Take the time to give your mind the chance to become still. Use deep breaths to achieve this state of relaxation.

Second, become aware of your question or concern.

Third, clearly tell Spirit what sign will be a 'yes' answer and what sign you wish for 'no' answer.

If you are using a coin, decide which side is a 'yes' and which side is a 'no'.
If you are using a pendulum, ask the pendulum to show you a 'yes' movement and a 'no' movement.

You can also request a particular sign to help answer your yes /no questions. For example, you can ask, "If I see a deer, it means yes". If you see the deer you have a yes answer, if not, then your answer is no. You can also ask Spirit and/or Your Higher Self, what a 'yes' and 'no' signal would be for you.

Books

Randomly opening a book, preferably a spiritual book with which you feel aligned, is an easy method when seeking answers.

Relax and place your intention. Be very clear about your reasons for asking for a sign, such as, "What is my message for the day?"

Close your eyes and randomly open the book to whichever page feels right to you. Then as you move your fingers along the page, sense a place to stop and open your eyes to read what is below your fingers, the spot you randomly chose.

Tarot and Angel Cards

These cards connect the meaning within each card to the connection of our intuition and Higher Self. So many times the cards we turn over just so happen to make perfect sense with regard to whatever our current question and/or situation may be.

Sights and Sounds are Gentle Encouragements

Just observe the Sights and Sounds as gentle encouragement and support from the Universe, your Higher Self, your Guides and Angels. Trust your inner knowing when you are making your choices. You will know what is best for you. Always remember, there are no mistakes, just lessons to be learned.

Understanding the Sights and Sounds

1. Trust Your Intuition.
Believe in yourself and trust what first comes to your mind. Ask yourself what you were thinking or feeling just before you saw the Sight or heard the Sound.

2. Develop a Sights and Sounds Dictionary.
Keep track of the Sights and Sounds. Write them down and refer back to your writings if the Sights and Sounds occur again. Watch for patterns. As you become more comfortable and connected to your Higher Self and Spirit Guides, ask them for information about the Sights and Sounds that appear in your life. You can request further concrete insight as to the meaning and messages in the Sights and Sounds that you observe or that gain your attention.

3. Refer to a Sign Dictionary.
A Sign Dictionary can be a beginning to assist you to understand the meaning of the Sights and Sounds.

You are the one who really knows the true meaning of this sighting for yourself. Choose a meaning that makes sense to you. You will be attracted to the correct meaning for you. As you continue your practice of Spiritual Communication and the development of your Psychic centers you will come to establish a dialogue with Your Higher Self and Spirit and together you will discover a language that you both understand.

(More information can be found in the book, "The Secret Language of Signs" by Denise Linn)

.

CHAPTER FIFTEEN

Mirabai Devi's Energy Tools

Since the first edition of this book in 2006, I have been introduced to Mirabai Devi, who has become my Spiritual Teacher and mentor in her Lightworker Program. Working with Mirabai for both my personal healing and awareness of working with The Divine Light, has changed my life in many, many ways.

I would like to share with you the tools of spiritual practice and energetic clearing that I have learned from working with Mirabai in her Lightworker and Apprenticeship programs.

Mirabai Devi is an international spiritual teacher, conduit for healing, author, and the founder of the *Mirabai Devi Foundation*. The Foundation is dedicated to her mission of raising world consciousness through the awakening and healing of humanity.
www.mirabidevi.org

Mirabai teaches that The Divine Light does all the work. The Light does all the healing, teaching, guiding and informing. All we have to do is ask. Ask for the help of The Light and allow It to do the work of clearing, balancing, healing, whatever is appropriate for you and for any situation.

And so, we ask, allow and, very importantly, give thanks and extend gratitude for the help of The Divine Light.

Here are the tools that are highly recommended to assist energy workers/healers.

Use of Mantra for removing Disharmonious energies, and also Mantras for Healing.

Forgiveness Prayers by Howard Wills.

Mirabai has produced guided meditation CDs to help us connect with The Divine Light, to learn about forgiveness and abundance.

The Divine Light CD
Ishta Devata CD
Abundance CD
Forgiveness CD

Mirabai has also produced CDs of instructional and inspirational talks that she has given at darshans, and Lightworker trainings.

Mirabai has authored a book, "Samadhi"
In which she has captured the insights and truths that have come to her during these enlightenment experiences in the form of short texts designed to by-pass the busy lower mind and awaken our deeper inner knowing. They are best pondered as meditations, allowing the truths to radiate within.

Recommended Reading

Below is a brief list of some of the many wonderful books I have discovered on my own journey on this spiritual path. Please feel free to choose whatever books may "speak" personally to you.

Angel Numbers 101, Doreen Virtue

Animal Speak, Ted Andrews, Llewellyn Publications

Autobiography of a Yogi, Paramahansa Yogananda

Become the Most Important Person in the Room, Your 30 Day Plan for Empath Empowerment, Rose Rosetree

Chakra Clearing, Doreen Virtue, Hay House

Empowered by Empathy – Rose Rosetree

Healing With The Angels, Doreen Virtue, Hay House

Heaven and Earth, James Van Praagh, Simon & Schuster

Plan Your Home With Feng Shui, Ian Bruce, Quantum

Proof of Heaven, Eben Alexander

Protected by the Light, Dr. Bruce Goldberg, Hats Off Publisher

Psychic Development for Beginners, William W. Hewitt, Llewellyn Publications

Sacred Space, Denise Linn, Ballantine Books

Spirit Allies, Christopher Penzack

The Care and Feeding of Indigo Children, Doreen Virtue

The Indigo Children, by Lee Carroll and Jan Tober

The Key, Echo Bodine

The Lightworkers Way, Doreen Virtue

The Secret Language of Signs, Denise Linn, Ballantine Books

The Unmistakeable Touch of Grace, Cheryl Richardson, Free Press

The Western Guide to Feng Shui, Terah Kathryn Collins, Hay House

Through The Darkness, Janet Nohavec

What Tom Sawyer Learned from Dying, Sidney Farr

Where Two Worlds Meet, Janet Nohavec

You are Psychic, Pete A. Sanders, Jr. Fawcett Columbine Book

Recommended Music

Below is some of my favorite music to meditate or simply relax to. Again, feel free to experiment with the many varieties to discover what works best for you.

Angel Love by Aeoliah

Atlantis Healing Temple Valley of the Sun, Box 38 Malibu, CA 90265

Bliss, Om Namah Shivaya II Robert Gass,

Creation, David Young

Crystal Bowl Healing, Steven Halpern

Crystal Bowl Sound Healing, Alchemy Bowls , Tryshe Dhevney

Diamonds in the Sun, Girish

Drumming to Journey By, Kay Cordell Whitaker

Eternal Om, Dick Sutphen

In Medicine River, Coyote Oldman,

Inner Peace, Steven Halpern

Jewels of Silence, by Ashana

Journey to the Temple 7 chakras, Llewellyn

Lumen De Lumine – Light of Light, Joseph Michael Levry,

Mantra for Healing : Ancient Chant Healing and Peace

Mantras for Precarious Times , Deva Premal

Ra Ma Da Sa, Healing Sound, Joseph Michael Levy,

Whale Meditation, Kamal

Satsang, **A Meditation in Song and Silence** Deva Premal and Miten

Seeds of Awakening, Guided Meditations - Self-Attunements for Remembering with your Higher Self, Gerri Shanti DeSimone, www.findpeacewithin.com

Shri Ram On Wings of Song by Robert Gass,

The Silent Path, Robert Haig Coxon ,

The Way of the Dolphin, Medwyn Goodall

This Universe, Singh Kaur

Recommended Guided Meditations

Abundance, Mirabai Devi

Chakra Clearing, Doreen Virtue, Helps you to clear and cleanse, energize and align your chakra centers.

Find Peace Within, A Journey of Remembering, Gerri DeSimone and Matt Pavolaitis, guided meditations

Forgiveness, Mirabai Devi

Healing For Healers, Karla McLaren, How to give without giving it all away. In this tape, Karla presents a completely grounded body-based meditative practice for the maintenance of your subtle energy body, your healing practice, and you.

Healing Your Aura & Chakras, Karla McLaren, www. Miode.com In this tape, Karla presents a body-based centering process that makes aura and chakra work simple and natural. She provides step-by-step explanations, and a complete healing for your aura, your chakra, and you.

Healing Journey, Marci Archambeault's beautiful, soothing voice leads you on a journey that heals the problems and pains of your past, frees you of the addiction in your life, and brings you to remember the perfection and beauty within yourself. The Quest, P.O.Box 54 Lunenberg, MA, 01462
(Marci has a number of guided meditations to offer you.)

Invocation of the Angels, Joan Borysenko, Ph.D, www.HayHouse.com On this tape Joan shares an ancient meditation with you, in which she invokes the help of four archangels and asks for their assistance in leading a kind, loving life. *Remember, You are Never Alone!*

Ishata Devata, The Divine Form, Mirabai Devi

Karma Releasing, Doreen Virtue, www.hayhouse.com
Helps you heal childhood and early adulthood wounds from this
life.

Manifesting with the Angels, Doreen Virtue,
Allowing Heaven to help you Fulfill Your Life's Purpose

Meditations, Shakti Gawain, New World Library, Navato, CA
94949 (4 meditations included in a set. Contacting Your Inner
Guide, Discovering Your Inner Child, Expressing Your Creative
Being, The Male and Female Within)

Meditations for Manifesting, Dr. Wayne W. Dyer,

Past Life Regressions with the Angels, Doreen Virtue,
Doreen helps you unwind and relax with a beautiful meditation
so that your unconscious mind can reveal its ancient secrets.

Photon Light Meditation, Omni Pure

Seeds of Awakening, Self Attunements for Connecting with
Your Higher Self. 6 Guided Meditations to cleanse, clear and
balance and attune your chakra system.
 Gerri Shanti DeSimone and Matt Pavolaitis,
www.findpeacewithin.com

The Golden Light, Guided Meditation by Mirabai Devi

NOTES

www.ingramcontent.com/pod-product-compliance
Lightning Source LLC
LaVergne TN
LVHW051154080426
835508LV00021B/2630